TITLES OF JESUS

A manual for prayer and praise based on New Testament titles of Our Lord, Jesus Christ.

Michael Scanlan, T.O.R.

Franciscan University Press
Steubenville, Ohio

DEDICATION

To Bill and Lu Kepler who supplied
the sanctuary in which this book
was written and to all their fellow
Christians on Maui who seek unity
in the Lordship of Jesus.

Approved: Very Rev. Dennis L. Sullivan,
        T.O.R., Minister Provincial

Cover: Photograph of a stained glass
   window in San Marco Catholic Church,
   Marco Island, Florida.

   Window design: Kate White Shulok,
      White Stained Glass Studio, Inc.,
      Sarasota, Florida.

   Photograph: John Cress, Cress
      Photography, Sarasota, Florida.

Cover Design: Art Mancuso

Inside Graphics: Colleen Johnson

Copyright © 1985, 1989
Franciscan University Press
All Rights Reserved.

Available from: Franciscan University Press
                University of Steubenville
                Steubenville, OH 43952

Printed in the United States of America

ISBN 0-940535-02-5

INTRODUCTION

There is a hidden treasure in the titles of Jesus. They are a resource for prayer, praise, and the renewal of our minds. So frequently, we fail to keep growing in our understanding of who Jesus is and, therefore, don't grow in our praise of Him.

In Philippians, Chapter 2, Paul proclaims the preeminence of Jesus:

> Therefore, God exalted him to the highest place and gave him the name that is above every name, that at the name of Jesus every knee should bow in heaven and on earth and every tongue confess that Jesus Christ is Lord, to the glory of the Father.

This great hymn of praise calls us to focus our lives on Jesus and to realize that the more we exalt who Jesus is and the more we praise his name, the more we glorify God. The Father is glorified as we exalt Jesus. And Jesus said of the Holy Spirit, "When he comes he will glorify me" (John 16:14).

We need to exalt Jesus with an ever deepening appreciation of who He is and what He has done for us. Paul exuberantly tells us that nothing can separate us from the love of Christ and that we can never plumb the depths or heights of who this Christ is. Paul used many titles for Jesus to express some of this height and depth. The writer of Hebrews used many more titles and the early christians delighted in using these titles to exalt different aspects of Jesus "for in Him all the fulness of God was pleased to dwell."

Gregory of Nyssa, a great Christian, wrote: "Paul calls Christ by many other titles too numerous to recall. Their cumulative force will give some conception of the marvelous content of the name of Christ, revealing to us his inexpressible majesty insofar as our minds and thoughts can comprehend it."

In my own life I began using the titles following a period when I found it difficult to praise God with fervor. I remember searching my mind and asking the Holy Spirit to inspire me.

The title **Faithful Witness** came to mind. I experienced a surge of power as I proclaimed it. I repeated it each time with

4

more fervor. I then added **Captain of Our Salvation**. Again, I experienced the anointing of the Spirit. In the following days I added other titles. I preached on the power of the titles of Jesus to our students. Finally, I decided to study all the titles and organize them for prayer purposes.

This booklet is called a manual because it is meant to be used actively, not merely read. Its purpose is to equip the user with a tool for prayer and praise. In order to make the manual as practical as possible, I decided on two limitations: 1) I would not include all the possible titles; 2) I would not attempt to give the full extent of the scriptures quoted or even the biblical background to the words used. I will explain how the decisions on these limitations were made.

I chose the titles by the following criteria: 1) I excluded Old Testament titles since my attempt was to concentrate on those titles that the New Testament upholds for worship, specifically of Jesus rather than of Yahweh; 2) Normally, I did not include synonyms as separate titles though, if they are part of the same scripture passage, they are included under the primary title; 3) I gave greater priority to using a title if a New

Testament writer set it off as an attribute of Jesus and finally; 4) My Franciscan brothers and I have been using these titles in praise for approximately two years and our sense is that certain titles have a deeper anointing for prayer and praise than others. This, of course, is subjective so I have allowed for some open pages at the end of the manual for the reader to add additional titles to the fifty-two developed here.

Secondly, the brief format I chose provided still another limitation. For each title, I cite the Scripture passage, give a key thought on it, follow this with a prayer, a decision and a petition. Each of these could be expanded greatly but, then there would be so many words that the booklet would not be a manual designed for repeated use. Instead, the scripture is confined to one passage and that only a brief excerpt; the key thought is a single insight without background development; the prayer is a simple response, normally of thanksgiving or praise; and the decision is a simple commitment which everyone can make for daily living. Finally, on each page there is a line for petition. The petition begins: "Come Lord Jesus." In many cases this is sufficient; we pray for the Lord to reign now in our lives and for the hastening of the return of the

Lord. Where the title and responses have stirred up additional needs for God's blessings these can be added to this basic petition. For this purpose the petition is followed by dots.

The Scripture verses have been translated directly from the Greek, but with reference to seven well established versions: **New American, New English, New International, Revised Standard, Jerusalem, Confraternity,** and **King James**. The purpose has been to arrive at a true translation which also reflects traditional phraseology used for worship.

HOW TO USE THE MANUAL

How should you use the manual? Use it in the way that most helps you to pray. Here are some suggestions that you can use alone, alternately, or in various combinations:

1) Familiarize yourself with the titles and repeat them daily to worship the Lord.

2) Develop one title each day as a point of prayer. Ask the Holy Spirit to reveal to you the depth of meaning of the title. Look up the full scripture passages.

3) Select a rotation of fifty-two weeks and deepen your appreciation of one title each week. Or, you may wish to select a fifty-two day rotation period.

4) Memorize the titles using the alphabetic order to fix them in your mind and frequently, at least daily, use them in praise.

LIST OF TITLES

ADVOCATE

Scripture: 1 John 2:1

> *If anyone does sin we have an*
> ***advocate*** *with the Father, Jesus Christ*
> *the Righteous One.*

Key Thought: Jesus takes our case,
represents us before the Father, pays
the price for our redemption from
sin, and intercedes for us at the
right hand of the Father.

Prayer Response: Thank you Lord for
being our **advocate**. We praise your
Holy Name.

Decision: I will be more trusting and con-
fident because Jesus is interceding
for me.

Petition: Come Lord Jesus. . . .

the AMEN

Scripture: Revelations 3:14

> *These things say **the Amen**, the faithful and true witness, the ruler of God's creation.*

Key Thought: Jesus was **the Amen,** the yes to the Father's plan. He willingly became man, suffered and died on the Cross because that was His Father's will for him.

Prayer Response: O Lord, thank you for your Amen. I commit myself to follow you in saying yes to God's plan for my life.

Decision: I will say yes to what God's will is for my life today.

Petition: Come Lord Jesus. . . .

APOSTLE OF OUR PROFESSION

Scripture: Hebrews 3:1

> *Therefore holy brethen who share in the heavenly calling, consider Jesus the High Priest and* **Apostle of our Profession**.

Key Thought: Jesus first gave his life as the Son of His Father, professing His faith, trusting all things into the Father's hands. He showed us the way and earned us the power and right to profess our faith as He did.

Prayer Reponse: Thank you Lord for going ahead of us, showing us the way to live and making it possible for us to follow. We praise you Lord for being faithful to all you professed.

Decision: I will profess my faith daily and strive to be faithful to all I profess.

Petition: Come Lord Jesus. . . .

AUTHOR AND FINISHER OF OUR FAITH

Scripture: Hebrews 12:2

> *Let us look to Jesus, the **author and finisher of our faith** who for the joy set before him endured the cross, despising the shame and sat down at the right hand of the throne of God.*

Key Thought: We would never be Christians with christian faith but for Jesus who first lived as the Father calls us to live. He showed us how to start and how to finish our life with God.

Prayer Response: O Lord, we thank you for our faith. We praise you for the example you gave us.

Decision: I will treasure the gift of faith Jesus won for me.

Petition: Come Lord Jesus. . . .

AUTHOR OF LIFE

Scripture: Acts 3:15

> *You killed the **Author of Life** but God raised him from the dead. To this we are witnesses.*

Key Thought: An author brings something into existence. Jesus, as **Author of Life**, brings into existence for us eternal life with God. He frees us from the sentence of death and offers us life.

Prayer Response: We thank you, Lord, for giving us life. We praise you with our new life in you.

Decision: I will live today as a Christian who knows new life and has no home in those things that share in spiritual death.

Petition: Come Lord Jesus. . . .

THE BEGINNING AND THE END
The Alpha and Omega
The First and the Last

Scripture: Revelations 22:13

*I am the Alpha and the Omega, the First and the Last, **the Beginning and the End**.*

Key Thought: All good begins and ends with Jesus. "In the beginning was the Word" (John 1:1). The final action in the history of the world will be Jesus' handing the Kingdom over to the Father. In the history of our personal lives, salvation begins with Jesus and ends with our standing before him who is our judge.

Prayer Response: O Lord, you are **the Beginning and the End**, the First and the Last, the Alpha and the Omega and we praise and thank you for this threefold title. Holy, Holy, Holy is the Lord.

Decision: I will begin and end each day with prayer and praise of Jesus.

Petition: Come Lord Jesus. . . .

BLESSED AND ONLY RULER

Scripture: 1 Timothy 6:14-16

> *I charge you to keep this commandment unstained and blameless until the appearing of our Lord Jesus Christ, which God will bring about in his own time. God, the **blessed and only ruler**, the King of Kings and Lord of Lords alone is immortal and lives in unapproachable light, Jesus, whom no one has seen or can see. To Him be honor and might forever. Amen.*

Key Thought: Jesus has been given all authority. He is, over all the rulers of the earth, blessed by God's authority. He can come and take full dominion at any time.

Prayer Response: We praise you, O Lord in your full authority and power and we proclaim, come Lord Jesus and reign.

Decision: Today I will trust in the Lord and not in the leaders of earthly governments. I will have confidence that the Lord controls everything.

Petition: Come Lord Jesus. . . .

BREAD OF LIFE

Scripture: John 6:35

> *Then Jesus said to them, "I am the bread of life."*

Key Thought: If we are to be spiritually alive we are to be nourished by Jesus and His Word.

Prayer Response: Lord, thank you for nourishing me and giving me life in you.

Decision: I will make certain that my principle concern for nourishment today is the Lord and his Word.

Petition: Come Lord Jesus. . . .

18

CAPTAIN OF SALVATION

Scripture: Hebrews 2:10

> *In bringing many sons to glory, it was fitting that God for whom and through whom everything exists, to perfect through suffering the **captain of their salvation**.*

Key Thought: Jesus not only won salvation for us but he is the captain of all who follow as his disciples. He has led the way and continues to intercede at the right hand of the Father for all his followers.

Prayer Response: Thank you Lord for your great gift of salvation and new life; thank you for not abandoning us but continuing to lead us into glory.

Decision: Today, I will strive to be a faithful follower of the Lord, the Captain of my Salvation.

Petition: Come Lord Jesus. . . .

CHIEF CORNERSTONE

Scripture: Ephesians 2:19-21

> *Consequently, you are no longer foreigners and aliens but fellow citizens with God's people and members of God's household built on the foundation of the apostles and prophets with Christ Jesus himself being the **Chief Cornerstone**. (cf: 1 Peter 2:6)*

Key Thought: Christians are not to be drifters following this or that person in this or that place. We are part of God's family, God's household which is firmly placed and rooted in Christ Jesus as the cornerstone upon which everything is built.

Prayer Response: O Lord, thank you for your gift to us of family and household. We praise you for your provision in our lives as Church, as Apostles and prophets and as brothers and sisters.

Decision: Today I will see my identity above all else as belonging to the household of God.

Petition: Come Lord Jesus. . . .

CHIEF SHEPHERD

Scripture: 1 Peter 5:4

And when the Chief Shepherd appears, you will receive the unfading crown of Glory.

Key Thought: Many are called to pastor and shepherd God's people but above all is the **Chief Shepherd** who guides the pastors in their care for his people. On the final day, other pastors will cease their shepherding as the **Chief Shepherd** appears to take his people to the Father.

Prayer Response: O Lord, thank you for being our shepherd, for caring for us and for leading us. We praise you for your constant provision in our lives.

Decision: Today I will submit my whole life recommitted to the Chief Shepherd and to whomever the Lord has established in pastoral care over me.

Petition: Come Lord Jesus. . . .

CHRIST

Scripture: John 1:41

> *Andrew first found his brother Simon and said to him, "We have found the Messiah," which means, the **Christ**.*

Key Thought: Christ means "the anointed one." Andrew concludes that Jesus is the Anointed One of God, anointed to save the people. He boldly announces this good news of discovering the **Christ** to his brother.

Prayer Response: Lord, we thank you for being our Messiah and **Christ**. We praise you.

Decision: Today, I will be bold in speaking of the Lord and I will seek to follow what God has anointed as his will for my life.

Petition: Come Lord Jesus. . . .

DAYSTAR

Scripture: 2 Peter 1:19

> *We have the prophetic word made more certain, and you will do well to pay attention to it as to a light shining in a dark place, until the day dawns and the **daystar** rises in the your hearts.*

Key Thought: Matthew 2:2 tells us that the magi saw "his star in the East and have come to worship him." The star of Jesus led them to Jesus. Jesus is our guiding star to lead us as children of the light.

Prayer Response: O Lord, we praise you for lighting our way.

Decision: I will seek the Lord's way and the Lord's mind today for all I do.

Petition: Come Lord Jesus. . . .

DELIVERER

Scripture: Romans 11:26

> *And so all Israel will be saved as it is written: "The **Deliverer** will come from Zion. He will banish godlessness from Jacob."*

Key Thought: We were in bondage to sin and Satan, having no merit of our own. Jesus delivered us from this bondage.

Prayer Response: We thank you and praise you, Lord, for your great action of rescuing and delivering us.

Decision: I will live today in gratitude for the Lord's having delivered me.

Petition: Come Lord Jesus. . . .

EMMANUEL
God is with us

Scripture: Matthew 1:23

> *The virgin will be with child and give birth to a son, and they will call him Emmanuel, a name which means God with us.*

Key Thought: Our security should not depend on having money, job, reputation or influential friends, but rather on having God with us. He who is with God triumphs and lives forever in God's glory.

Prayer Response: We praise you Lord for you are **Emmanuel** — not a distant or elusive god but God who has joined the human race and taken us unto himself.

Decision: Today, I will trust the Lord with my life for He is both present and committed to what is best for me.

Petition: Come Lord Jesus. . . .

ETERNAL LIFE

Scripture: 1 John 5:20

> *This is the true God and **eternal
> life**.*

Key Thought: Our relationships with
others can enhance our life, but
only one, Jesus Christ, is **eternal
life** for us.

Prayer Response: We praise you Lord
for your life. The life you give is
forever.

Decision: Today I will decide for eternal
life and not for passing pleasures.

Petition: Come Lord Jesus. . . .

FAITHFUL AND TRUE

Scripture: Revelations 19:11

> *I saw the heavens opened and, I beheld a white horse, whose rider is called* **Faithful and True**.

Key Thought: In our lives we deal constantly with our failure to be faithful to our commitments. We wrestle with our compromises, our exaggerations, and our misleadings. Jesus, however, was totally faithful to the Father and absolutely filled with truth in all he said or did.

Prayer Response: We praise you Lord for you are the standard of what is faithful and true.

Decision: Today I will strive to be faithful in all I do and truthful in all I say.

Petition: Come Lord Jesus. . . .

FAITHFUL WITNESS

Scripture: Revelations 1:4-5

> *Grace to you and peace from Him who is and who was and who is to come, and from the seven spirits before his throne, and from Jesus Christ, who is the **faithful witness**. . . .*

Key Thought: Jesus gave witness to who God is and to God's plan for our salvation. He is absolutely faithful in what he witnesses and he is totally trustworthy. We can stake our lives on these truths.

Prayer Response: Thank you Lord for being faithful to the Father in all things. We praise you for your witness to us.

Decision: Today, I will imitate the Lord and strive to witness to others the truth and love of God.

Petition: Come Lord Jesus. . . .

FIRST-BORN OF THE DEAD

Scripture: Colossians 1:18

> *And he is the head of the body, the church; he is the beginning, the **first-born of the dead**, so that in all things he might be preeminent.*

Key Thought: Through sin we all died. We did not have eternal life. Jesus became man and joined human nature to eternal life. He died and rose from the dead so that we too can be born from the dead.

Prayer Response: Lord, we thank you and praise you for being born among us and bringing us eternal life.

Decision: Today I will live as a reborn Christian, conscious of the gift of eternal life.

Petition: Come Lord Jesus. . . .

GOOD SHEPHERD

Scripture: John 10:11-14

> *I am the **good shepherd**. The good shepherd lays down his life for His sheep . . . I am the **good shepherd**; I know mine and mine know me, just as the Father knows me and I know the Father, and I lay down my life for the sheep.*

Key Thought: Jesus cares for us as a shepherd who is willing to die to save one of his sheep. Jesus did die for us and he won't abandon us now. We can know him and be at peace in his care.

Prayer Response: Thank you Lord for your love and care. We praise you as our **Good Shepherd**.

Decision: Today I will put my trust in the Lord, the Good Shepherd.

Petition: Come Lord Jesus . . . .

GREAT HIGH PRIEST

Scripture: Hebrews 4:14

> *Therefore since we have a **great high priest** having gone through the heavens, Jesus the Son of God, let us hold firmly to the faith we profess.*

Key Thought: Priests are called to stand as mediators between God and his people offering sacrifices to God on behalf of the people. Jesus is the **Great High Priest** who offered the sacrifice of his life for us and continues to offer that sacrifice in intercession for us.

Prayer Response: Thank you O Lord for paying the price of our redemption. We praise you Lord as our **Great High Priest**.

Decision: Today I will intercede for the needs of those in my care by joining my prayers to the sacrifices of Jesus, our High Priest.

Petition: Come Lord Jesus. . . .

HEAD OF THE CHURCH

Scripture: Ephesians 5:23

> . . . *Christ is the* **head of the Church**, *his body, and is Himself its Savior* . . . *And he is the head of the body, the Church* (Col 1:18).

Key Thought: As our physical bodies follow the directions of our heads which control all our actions, so Jesus, as the Head of his body, the Church, should direct and lead all its members.

Prayer Response: Lord, reign over my life and the life of your whole Church.

Decision: Today I will seek to submit everything in my life to the direction of Jesus, the Lord and Head of the Church.

Petition: Come Lord Jesus. . . .

HOPE OF GLORY

Scripture: Colossians 1:27

> *To them God willed to make known among the Gentiles the glorious riches of this mystery which is Christ in you, the **hope of Glory**.*

Key Thought: We want many things, but in particular, eternal happiness. In Christ we can confidently hope for this Glory.

Prayer Response: We thank you Lord for the hope poured in our hearts by your Spirit, a hope that will not disappoint.

Decision: Today I will live in hope based on the gift of the Risen Lord to me.

Petition: Come, Lord Jesus. . . .

I AM

Scripture: John 8:58

> *"I tell you the truth," Jesus answered, "before Abraham was born, **I am**."*

Key Thought: The Word of God, the Son took on human nature and became man. But the Word, the Son was from the beginning, for He is God. Therefore His existence has always been and is not subject to time.

Prayer Response: We praise You eternal Lord, the **I Am**, whose existence always has been, is and always will be now and forever. Amen.

Decision: Today I will strive to see more with the mind of God and view this world as passing away, but the Lord as remaining forever.

Petition: Come Lord Jesus. . . .

JESUS CHRIST OUR LORD

Scripture: Romans 1:4

> . . . *who through the Spirit of holiness was declared with power to be the Son of God by his resurrection from the dead:* **Jesus Christ our Lord**.

Key Thought: "Jesus" means the one who saves. "Christ" means the anointed one. "Lord" means the ruler and "our Lord" means he rules over us. Together we have proclaimed a savior anointed by God to reign for us and over us.

Prayer Response: We praise you Lord in the fulness of who you are.

Decision: Today, I will live in the reality that the greatest man who ever lived is given to us and for us.

Petition: Come, Lord Jesus. . . .

JUST ONE
Righteous one

Scripture: 1 John 2:1 (cf: Acts 7:52)

> *But if anybody does sin, we have an advocate with the Father in our defense — Jesus Christ, the Just One.*

Key Thought: There is only one person who is fully just and righteous on his own merits: the Lord Jesus Christ and He intercedes for us so that our sins will be forgiven.

Prayer Response: Lord you indeed are just, righteous and holy. We praise you for who you are and for what you have done for us.

Decision: Whenever I sin, I will not delay to repent and receive God's forgiveness for I know the Just One has earned it for me.

Petition: Come, Lord Jesus. . . .

KING OF KINGS AND LORD OF LORDS

Scripture: 1 Timothy 6:14-16

*I charge you to keep this command-ment unstained and without reproach until the appearance of our Lord Jesus Christ, which God will bring about in his own time — God, the blessed and only Ruler; the **King of Kings** and **Lord of lords** who alone is immortal and who lives in unapproachable light, whom no one has seen or can see. To Him be honor and might forever. Amen*

Key Thought: No power or honor is greater than the power and majesty of our Lord.

Prayer Response: "To Him be honor and might forever. Amen."

Decision: Today I shall not fear. I will praise my Lord and trust in Him.

Petition: Come, Lord Jesus. . . .

LAMB OF GOD

Scripture: John 1:29

> The next day he saw Jesus coming toward him and said, "Behold, the **Lamb of God**, who takes away the sin of the world!"

Key Thought: Jesus was sacrificed on the cross for us as lambs were sacrificed in reparation for sin to God. Now it is God initiating the sacrifice of His Son for our sins.

Prayer Response: Thank you Lord for embracing the cross and sacrificing your life for us in love.

Decision: Today I will live in a manner worthy of the Lord's sacrifice for me.

Petition: Come, Lord Jesus. . . .

LIGHT OF THE WORLD

Scripture: John 8:12

> *Again Jesus spoke to them. He said,
> "I am the **light of the world**. Who-
> ever follows me will not walk in dark-
> ness, but will have the light of life."*

Key Thought: We live in darkness, not
seeing the true meaning of life until
we know Jesus and follow him.

Prayer Response: Thank you Lord for
lighting our way.

Decision: Today I will choose to walk in
the light of faith according to the
gospel.

Petition: Come, Lord Jesus. . . .

LION OF JUDAH

Scripture: Revelation 5:5

> *Then one of the elders said to me, "Do not cry! Behold, the **Lion of the tribe of Judah**, the Root of David has overcome."*

Key Thought: Jesus has triumphed over sin and death. He is the worthy one, worthy to lead us into glory. He is a descendant of David, but one who conquers and reigns over all.

Prayer Response: We praise you Lord, **Lion of Judah**, the triumphant one.

Decision: Today I will thank the Lord for all he has done for me.

Petition: Come, Lord Jesus. . . .

LORD

Scripture: Philippians 2:10-11

> *So that at Jesus' name every knee must bend in the heavens on earth and under the earth, and every tongue proclaim to the glory of God, the Father: Jesus Christ is **Lord**.* (see also Lord of All, Acts 10:36)

Key Thought: The earliest anthem of Christianity was "Jesus is **Lord**." This was the proclamation of the new Christians as they discovered not just that Jesus had ultimate power over the powers of the earth as expressed in "King of Kings and Lord of Lords" but power for themselves personally. Jesus is **Lord** over the lives of all committed Christians and disciples of Christ.

Prayer Response: O Lord, you are **Lord** of my life and I praise you that you have called me to follow you.

Decision: Today I will act as one who serves a loving and all powerful Lord and therefore I cannot be hopeless or helpless.

Petition: Come, Lord Jesus. . . .

LORD GOD ALMIGHTY

Scripture: Revelations 4:8

> *And the four living creatures each of them with six wings and covered with eyes all around, even inside and day and night they never stop saying: "Holy, Holy, Holy is the **Lord God Almighty** who was, and is to come."*

Key Thought: Christ Jesus comprises it all: He is Lord, ruler of all that is, He is God having the divine nature; he is almighty, lacking nothing in might and power.

Prayer Response: We praise you our Lord; we join the angels and saints in proclaiming Holy, Holy, Holy, is the Lord God Almighty.

Decision: My highest praise today will go to the Lord who is above all that exists.

Petition: Come, Lord Jesus. . . .

MASTER

Scripture: John 13:13

> *You call me **master** and lord and rightly; so I am.*

Key Thought: **Master** in the sense of the Greek word means here that Jesus is rightly addressed as the teacher and director of the lives of his disciples. Jesus exercised direct authority to form the lives of those who fully committed themselves to be his disciples.

Prayer Response: Thank you Lord for being our **Master** and continuing to direct and guide our lives. You are indeed the Way, the Truth, and the Life for us.

Decision: I will submit the practical details and direction of my life to the Lord and to those he has called to care for me.

Petition: Come, Lord Jesus. . . .

MESSIAH

Scripture: John 1:41

> *Andrew first found his brother Simon and said to him, "We have found the **Messiah** (which means the Christ)."*

Key Thought: The Messiah was the longed for savior and redeemer of Israel who would free God's people from oppression. Finding the Messiah was a tremendous joy to any Jew who recognized him.

Prayer Response: We thank you Lord for being our **Messiah** and for being present whenever we seek after you.

Decision: I will rejoice today that I have found the one who gives me salvation and redemption.

Petition: Come, Lord Jesus. . . .

MORNING STAR

Scripture: Revelations 22:16

> *I am the Root and Offspring of David, the bright **Morning Star**.*

Key Thought: This is another term for Dayspring and Rising Sun but it has special power in giving us the image of a bright star to lead us as children of the light.

Prayer Response: O Lord, **Morning Star**, we thank you for leading us on our way.

Decision: Today I will follow the Lord and his ways in all that I do.

Petition: Come, Lord Jesus. . . .

NAZARENE

Scripture: Matthew 2:23

> *So was fulfilled what was spoken through the prophets: "He shall be called a **Nazarene**."*

Key Thought: Jesus was truly man, down to belonging to a specific and little known geographic area, Nazareth. He took on our nature as fully as he could.

Prayer Response: Lord you have walked this life before us. We thank you for bearing our nature and redeeming it.

Decision: Today I will renew my effort to follow the Lord in all I do.

Petition: Come, Lord Jesus. . . .

OFFSPRING OF DAVID

Scripture: Revelation 22:16

> *I am the Root and the **Offspring of David**. . . .*

Key Thought: We all descend from parents, grandparents, great grandparents and on back. We inherit physical characteristics, personality traits and the original sin of our first parents. Jesus was born in a line of descendants. He looked like an Israelite and kept the traditions of the House of David. He didn't inherit sin but took it on for us by becoming one of us. He joined the human race as fully as he could while still being God.

Prayer Response: We thank you Lord for becoming one of us and freeing us from the burden of sin we inherited.

Decision: Today I will model my behavior on Jesus. He became like me so that I might become like Him.

Petition: Come, Lord Jesus. . . .

OUR PASSOVER

Scripture: 1 Corinthians 5:7

> *For Christ **our Passover** — has been sacrificed.*

Key Thought: Jesus was the lamb which was sacrificed. He passed over from death to life. He is truly our passover sacrifice, winning life for us.

Prayer Response: We praise **Our Passover,** the Lamb of God.

Decision: Today I will embrace the sufferings of my life uniting them with the sacrifice of Jesus.

Petition: Come, Lord Jesus. . . .

POWER AND WISDOM OF GOD

Scripture: 1 Corinthians 1:24

> . . . *but to those whom God has called, both Jews and Greeks, Christ, the **Power and the Wisdom of God**.*

Key Thought: It was Jesus Christ who conquered sin and death. He is the **power** that overcomes the world, the flesh, and the devil and he is the **wisdom** who teaches and leads all who would follow to everlasting life and glory.

Prayer Response: We praise you, conquering Jesus. We thank you that you are God's **power** and **wisdom** for our lives.

Decision: I will trust the Lord today, knowing His power is over all.

Petition: Come, Lord Jesus. . . .

RABBI

Scripture: John 1:49

> *Then Nathaniel answered, "**Rabbi** you are the Son of God; you are the King of Israel."*

Key Thought: Jesus was a Jew and a teacher, properly called **Rabbi**. We honor Him in his humanity and his authority over us by calling Him **Rabbi**.

Prayer Response: We thank you Lord for you are our Teacher and **Rabbi**.

Decision: Today I will remember that I have been privileged to be taught by the master teacher of all.

Petition: Come, Lord Jesus. . . .

RESURRECTION AND LIFE

Scripture: John 11:25-26

> *Jesus said to her, "I am the **Resurrection and the Life**, the one believing in me will live even though he dies; and whoever lives and believes in me shall never die."*

Key Thought: Jesus is life. He conquered death and rose as the first-born of many brothers. When we attach ourselves to him in faith we rise to new life.

Prayer Response: We thank you Lord for you are the **Resurrection and Life**, and in you we have life.

Decision: I will not give in today to anxiety, despair or discouragement for these are the signs of death and I want to live my life in witness to the Resurrection and the Life.

Petition: Come, Lord Jesus. . . .

RISING SUN

Scripture: Luke 1:77-79

> . . . *through the tender mercy of our God by which the Rising Sun will come to us from on high to shine on those living in darkness and in the shadow of death, to guide our feet into the way of peace.*

Key Thought: In Zechariah's hymn Jesus is presented as the **Rising Sun**. He is the source from which the day springs. Because Jesus has come, God's people are able to see and can move from darkness into light, recognizing the path to reconciliation with God in peace.

Prayer Response: Thank you Lord for being our source of light and truth and for guiding us on our way.

Decision: I will start each day with prayer to the Lord that He show me how to live.

Petition: Come, Lord Jesus. . . .

RULER OF THE KINGS OF THE EARTH

Scripture: Revelations 1:5

> *Grace to you and peace from Him who is and who was and who is to come and from the seven spirits before his throne and from Jesus Christ who is the faithful witness, the first-born from the dead and the* **Ruler of the Kings of the Earth**.

Key Thought: Jesus rules over all the great leaders of the earth. He will come in His time to take full dominion.

Prayer Response: We praise you, O Lord, for your majesty. You are over all the rulers of the earth.

Decision: I will live today conscious that all things in this world end with Jesus Christ's coming again to rule over all the earth.

Petition: Come, Lord Jesus. . . .

SAVIOR

Scripture: Luke 2:11 (cf. 2 Peter 2:20)

> *For today in the town of David a*
> ***Savior*** *has been born to you; who is*
> *Christ the Lord.*

Key Thought: We could not save ourselves from the bondage and punishment due to sin. We were under a sentence of death. Jesus saved us more truly than any lifeguard ever saved a drowning child.

Prayer Response: We praise you **Savior** of all the people. Thank you for coming and rescuing us.

Decision: Today I will call upon the saving power of the Lord to protect me and rescue me from all that leads me to sin.

Petition: Come, Lord Jesus. . . .

SHEPHERD AND BISHOP OF SOULS

Scripture: 1 Peter 2:25

> *For you were as sheep wandering
> but now you have returned to the
> **Shepherd and Bishop of your souls**.*

Key Thought: Jesus is committed to the
highest good for us. He continues to
care for us even as we wander away
from God's plan just as a shepherd
seeks after a stray sheep. He over-
sees the development of our spiritual
life so that our souls have everything we need for salvation.

Prayer Response: Thank you Lord for
your love and care. Come Lord and
guide us home.

Decision: I will begin today by calling on
the Lord for He cares for my life.

Petition: Come, Lord Jesus. . . .

SON OF GOD
Son of the Blessed
(Mark 14:61)
Son of the Most High
(Luke 1:32)

Scripture: Matthew 26:63-64

> *The high priest said to him, "I charge you by the living God; tell us if you are Christ, the **Son of God**." Jesus said to him, "You have said it."*

Key Thought: Jesus knew who he was and answered directly the question of the high priest, even though Jesus knew it would mean death for himself.

Prayer Response: All praise, honor, and glory to you Christ, **Son of God**.

Decision: Today I will live as a son of God and be ready to testify that I have new life through the Son of God.

Petition: Come, Lord Jesus. . . .

SON OF MAN

Scripture: Matthew 26:64

> *But I say to you, hereafter you will see the **Son of Man** sitting on the right hand of the Power and coming on the clouds of heaven.*

Key Thought: Jesus regularly called himself the **Son of Man**. By that he affirmed not only his human nature but that he was the promised one, the **Son of Man** foretold by Daniel and the prophets. He has come and will come again.

Prayer Response: Lord you have found us so that you may lead us to the Father. Come and rule over your people.

Decision: Today I will focus on the great truth that the Lord will come again and gather His kingdom to present it to the Father.

Petition: Come, Lord Jesus. . . .

TEACHER

Scripture: Matthew 23:10

> *Nor be called teachers, for you have one **Teacher**, the Christ.*

Key Thought: Jesus came to teach us how to live. All others are called to base their teaching on what Jesus has revealed and to teach in the power of the Spirit of Jesus.

Prayer Response: Thank you Lord for being our **teacher** and showing us the way.

Decision: Today I will study the scriptures to learn better how to live.

Petition: Come, Lord Jesus. . . .

VINE

Scripture: John 15:1

> *I am the true **Vine** and my father is the vine-dresser.*

Key Thought: We only have life if we are connected to Jesus as a branch to a vine.

Prayer Response: Thank you Lord for giving us life and sustaining us each day.

Decision: Today I will cherish my life in Jesus above all else.

Petition: Come, Lord Jesus. . . .

WAY, TRUTH, AND LIFE

Scripture: John 14:6

> *Jesus said to him, "I am the **Way, the Truth, and the Life**. No one comes to the Father, except through me."*

Key Thought: Man seeks to know truth about everything, about the way to live, and about life without end. Jesus is the answer for these yearnings and the only answer to finding God.

Prayer Response: We thank you Lord for being all for us, our **way**, our **truth**, and our **life**.

Decision: Today I will live as one who has found the answer to life in Jesus.

Petition: Come, Lord Jesus. . . .

WORD OF GOD

Scripture: Revelations 19:13

*He is clothed in a garment dipped in blood, and the name by which he is called is the **Word of God**.*

Key Thought: "In the beginning was the Word." With this statement John begins his gospel. The **Word of God**, the Son of God was always existing. He is the full expression of the Father and He is coming again to bring the fullness of justice and truth.

Prayer Response: We praise you Lord, the **Word of God**. You have revealed God to us.

Decision: Today I will seek to know God better through His word.

Petition: Come, Lord Jesus. . . .

WORD OF LIFE

Scripture: 1 John 1:1

> *This is what we proclaim to you what was from the beginning, what we heard, what we have seen with our eyes, what we have looked upon and our hands have touched. We speak of the **Word of Life**.*

Key Thought: Jesus was so real that the witnesses in the Apostolic age could speak of hearing, seeing, and touching him. He is present to us in a different but just as real manner.

Prayer Response: We praise you Lord. You are true life and give life to all who come to you.

Decision: Today I choose life and not death. I will choose the way of the Lord, the Word of Life.

Petition: Come, Lord Jesus. . . .

Selected Old Testament Titles of Jesus which are useful for praise and worship.

Title	Scripture
Desire of all Nations	Haggai 2:7
Father-Forever	Isaiah 9:5
God-Hero	Isaiah 9:5
Holy One of Israel	Isaiah 41:14
Key of David	Isaiah 22:22
Lord Our Righteousness	Jeremiah 23:6
Man of Sorrows	Isaiah 53:3
Prince of Peace	Isaiah 9:6
Root of Jesse	Isaiah 11:10
Wonder-Counselor	Isaiah 9:5